the Suffragette View

the Suffragette View

Antonia Raeburn

David & Charles

Newton Abbot   London   Vancouver

To the many Suffragettes
who wished for the true spirit of
the Movement
to be preserved

With appreciation and thanks
for all their generous help.

A.R.

All illustrations in this book
come from the author's collection,
with the exception of that at the
foot of page 17, The Albert Hall
Disturbances, for which acknow-
ledgements are due to the British
Museum.

ISBN 0 7153 7034 0 ✓

Set in Plantin 10 on 11 pt
and printed in Great Britain
at the Alden Press, Oxford
for David & Charles (Holdings) Limited
South Devon House Newton Abbot Devon

Published in Canada
by Douglas David & Charles Limited
132 Philip Avenue North Vancouver BC

Contents

Foreword

One of the many pleasures of being old is the opportunity this affords for casting a sceptical eye on documentary presentations of the drama of our time. We who are old have the special dispensation of remembering distant experiences more clearly and vividly than recent ones. Thus, happenings which to the young are history – even, in the atmosphere of immediacy created by the media, sometimes quite remote history – to us seem to belong to yesterday. I find it most enjoyable in my seventies to check what pass for being historical accounts, written or spoken, or on film for the television screen, against my remembrance of the actuality. For instance, the Jarrow Hunger March, The General Strike, the Economic Depression of the late twenties and early thirties, and – the subject of this book – the origins, struggles and ultimate triumph of the Suffragette Movement. Let me say at once that, submitted to this test, Miss Raeburn's text and supporting illustrations provide an admirably cool, objective and at the same time sympathetic, picture of the suffragette scene as I remember it.

As it happens, though of course I was not personally involved, I do remember it very clearly; more so, in fact, than other ostensibly more significant happenings. There was a lot of talk about it in my suburban home, much of it ribald. My father, an early socialist, felt in duty bound to be theoretically in favour of Votes for Women, but in private conversation with his cronies treated the subject with a certain derision. I feel sure that he neither hoped nor expected they would get the vote in his lifetime. The same thing went for his cronies, who were all either fellow-socialists or socialist sympathisers. They were on the whole a very masculine lot, and spoke with scarcely veiled contempt of male supporters of the suffragettes like Pethick Lawrence. In my childhood mind I came to think of these as like hen-pecked husbands, and somehow identified them with Mr Pooter in *The Diary of a Nobody* – always a favourite character. At school we repeated smutty jokes about Mrs Pankhurst and her sisters-in-arms, and generally viewed facetiously what are now seen as the first stirrings of women's lib.

My impression is that in those days, apart from a relatively few dedicated zealots, most of whom were middle- or upper-class, Votes for Women was more a music-hall joke than a sacred cause. Take the case of my mother who had come straight from a working-class home in Sheffield. She was implacably opposed to female suffrage, didn't want the vote herself at any price, and considered that voting, like smoking, bicycling in bloomers and what was then called free-love, demeaned her sex. I remember being greatly surprised years later, when I became acquainted with Beatrice Webb, to find that she, too, had little enthusiasm for or belief in Votes for Women, considering – as she well might – that she had managed to make herself felt socially and politically very effectively without access to the ballot-box. In this she perhaps failed to take due account of the advantages she enjoyed, in throwing her weight about, in being married to Sydney. Had she become the wife of her first and greatest love, Joseph Chamberlain, she might have felt differently.

Then, in the years before the outbreak of the 1939–45 war, when I was making one of my periodic attempts to sever myself for ever from Fleet Street, I fell in with a little nest of suffragette veterans and their more youthful neophytes gathered round Lady Rhondda (Mrs Humphrey Mackworth), and the magazine *Time & Tide* which she founded, edited and directed. Hugh Kingsmill unkindly called it a waste-product of the Rhondda Valley. My own part in the magazine's running was to contribute book-reviews and, occasionally, stand in for the literary editor, Theodora Bosanquet, a lady with a deep voice and a moustache who had been Henry James's secretary. She was exceedingly kind and amusing, and I grew very fond of her. Lady Rhondda herself, in her suffragette days, had been an activist, and got herself arrested and briefly imprisoned. She was also reputed to have been subjected to forcible feeding, which in her case, given her burly physique and robust temperament, must have been quite a formidable operation. All this gave her great prestige in suffragette circles, and might be considered as the equivalent, among male war veterans, of three or four wound-stripes. With Lady Rhondda I met some of the survivors of the great campaigning days, and the office of *Time & Tide* itself had about it a flavour, if not, as I fancied, a slight aroma, of militant ladies prepared to shriek and scratch and kick for feminism.

When my friend Antonia Raeburn asked me to contribute a foreword to her book I felt bound to point out that my feelings about the suffragette movement were well this side of idolatry. Furthermore, that with the best will in the world I could not manage to persuade myself that the extension of the franchise generally over the last century and a half to take in pretty well everyone, women included, had noticeably served to ameliorate our human circumstances. Miss Raeburn was kind enough to consider this no impediment, and I was encouraged to proceed by noting that she herself emerges from her writings on the subject as being no more an unqualified protagonist of female suffrage than I am.

Rather, what she is concerned to show, as it seems to me, is that the suffragette leaders were quite remarkable women – which, indeed, they demonstrably were – that their followers displayed great courage and dedication, and that the tactics they employed, though derided at the time, proved singularly effective. This is borne out by the fact that they have been followed subsequently in all sorts of agitations and demonstrations, ranging between major operations like the Swaraj Movement in India, and small forays by student gangs against campus regulations which irk them and dons who displease them. In other words, the first suffragettes established a technique of dissent which has played a crucial role in this age's turbulence. In this sense, a Michael Collins, a Gandhi, a Kwame Nkrumah may be seen as standing on the shoulders of the suffragettes. I have a cherished memory of hearing at an early meeting of the Indian National Congress a cracked rendering of *The Wearin' o' the Green*. One of the suffragette songs would have been equally appropriate. Indeed, in the person of Mrs Annie Besant, a sometime congress president, the line of descent from Mrs Pankhurst was unmistakable.

In any case, it is not for me to draw a moral where Miss Raeburn herself has desisted. The agitation for Votes for Women, like many another in our time, may well have produced consequences which its initiators would have found distasteful. I cannot believe, for instance, that Germaine Greer would have been particularly acceptable to Lady Rhondda, or have easily gained access to the columns of *Time & Tide*. What, however, is incontrovertible is that, as Miss Raeburn shows, the suffragette movement stirred up in many a female breast a just indignation at being accorded only a subordinate position in our national life and politics, that it brought into public life women who would otherwise have languished in obscurity, and that it has been a crucial factor in the social history and *mores* of the twentieth century.

Malcolm Muggeridge

Introduction

Women have joined forces with women at various times throughout the history of the world, but there is no parallel with the British suffragette movement, which divided the whole nation as a bitter issue for nine years at the beginning of the present century. At the same time, the movement served to unite people of every class and from every part of the country in a way which changed their outlook on life and gave an entirely new concept of the capabilities of women. It was not a sex war, however; the women were fighting for increased status which they believed the vote would give them. Their greatest enemies were apathy, on the part of both men and women, and Asquith, the stubborn Liberal Prime Minister who was adamant that women should not have the vote.

It was the *Daily Mail* which invented the name 'suffragette' in 1906, when it became necessary to make a distinction between those intellectual suffragists who had been respectfully but unsuccessfully campaigning for the rights of women throughout the previous half century, and between the young interrupters of political meetings who had now startled the public into taking notice.

Previously a woman had no right to let her voice be heard at a political meeting. She was little more than a plaything or a drudge. Victorian society ensured that she would either be fully occupied as mistress of a vast household with all its intricacies, or she would be employed as a slave within a family, office or factory. As simplified living arrived with the Edwardian era, so women were left with far less to occupy them. This was due to increased mechanical efficiency and reaction against Victorian fussiness, for most probably the accumulation of knick-knacks, useless household effects, and the complicated Victorian *toilette* and etiquette was merely an excuse to keep women so occupied that they could not interfere with activities that men considered their indisputable province.

The vote was the means to an end, a general struggle to shake free from the old ties and for the 'new woman' to prove herself. It is remarkable that the young women at the turn of the century were of a different brand from their predecessors. Universal education had given them an opportunity to stretch themselves both mentally and physically. Women from every walk of life had eagerly absorbed the intellectual material now offered them for the first time, and it appears from constant press references to women's increased height, good looks and intelligence that there was indeed a notable change. By contrast we read of the 'mere man' and contemporary pictures prove that these references are not just a joke. The men were smaller in stature and also, as articles in the press of the time point out, fewer in number than the women.

It was safe to comment on these facts in 1903 when women still, in spite of their increased abilities, remained in abeyance. But what were those educated women – particularly the poorer women of the middle classes – to do with their lives ? A former suffragette explained that, 'there was nothing of any interest that women could do unless they happened to be daughters of very well-off families. Teaching was about the only thing that didn't cost an awful lot. Most girls tended to live at home and to help with the housework and marry – if they married – but many of them stayed spinsters'.

The typical 'superfluous woman', and she was the one who eventually joined with others to form the rank and file of the suffragette movement, might be a member of a large family or an only child. Very often she had lost either or both of her parents and, being thus deprived of social well-being, she was even more innocent of the ways of the world than she might otherwise have been. The recruits who proved most faithful to the suffragette movement came into it as people whom the world had left blank and who had themselves made no impression, either good or bad, on society. Also among the suffragette ranks were artists, writers and teachers; but, sympathetic as this type of semi-professional woman was, she tended, as a rule, to join one of the non-militant suffrage societies that rapidly sprung up as soon as the suffragettes had achieved some success. The Women's Social and Political Union (WSPU) was the one truly militant organisation, although the Women's Freedom League, a splinter group, also pledged itself to make active protest against any government which refused to consider votes for women.

The WSPU was by no means the first society to campaign for women's suffrage. The National Union of Women's Suffrage Societies had been running since 1861 and each of the leading political parties had affiliated women's societies. Their intellectual approach, though effective at first had, by 1900, made little progress towards furthering their cause. It was in 1903 that Mrs Pankhurst and two of her daughters, Christabel and Sylvia, founded the WSPU. Its main object was to be independent of any political party and to persuade electors to vote against any parliamentary candidate who refused to consider votes for women. It has often been said that the Pankhursts were born leaders. They were certainly ideally suited to carry out the strange role which they set themselves, and, though it is Mrs Pankhurst who has been given world-wide credit, she would have been unable to become the woman figurehead of the century without the support and inspiration which she received from her daughters.

Christabel Pankhurst

Sylvia Pankhurst

Left. Mrs Emmeline Pankhurst in 1906

Adela Pankhurst

Emmeline Pankhurst was born on 14 July 1858, the anniversary of the storming of the Bastille which, she felt, may have accounted for her passionate idealism. She was the eldest daughter of Robert Gouldon, a Manchester textile manufacturer and an ardent supporter of the anti-slavery campaign. At the age of twenty, after completing her education in France, Emmeline fell in love with Dr Richard Marsden Pankhurst, a Manchester barrister, twenty years older than herself and a radical politician. He had been a founder member of the first woman's suffrage society, and had drafted bills on behalf of women's emancipation. Although these were accepted and had included the successful Married Women's Property Act of 1882, his attempts to enter Parliament, first as a Liberal and later as a Labour candidate, were unsuccessful.

Mrs Pankhurst bore him five children but her first son, Frank, died at the age of four. This was the first of a series of tragic events which periodically scarred her life. However, in spite of financial pressures, the Pankhursts, although somewhat eccentric by conventional standards, were a most happy and devoted family. The children were brought up to appreciate art and literature, but politics played the all-important part in their lives. At a very early age they attended political meetings and shared their parents' enthusiasm for reform. Mrs Pankhurst felt that as a woman she had a very definite contribution to make towards the welfare of society, and as soon as her children were old enough she applied to the Manchester Board of Guardians and was elected to serve on their committee whose business it was to organise the proper running of the Workhouse. In this capacity she came face to face with the terrible conditions suffered by the under-privileged and the poor, and she realised how little could be done to relieve the situation when men in power were totally unconcerned.

In 1898 a new tragedy put an end to the Pankhursts' happy home life. Dr Pankhurst suddenly died, leaving his widow to provide for the family. Harry, the youngest child, was then only eight years old; Adela twelve; and Sylvia and Christabel fifteen and seventeen. Mrs Pankhurst, after a short and unsuccessful attempt to run a fancy-goods business, was appointed Registrar of Births and Deaths for the Chorlton upon Medlock Sub-District of Manchester. Once again she saw the problems of society at first hand, and her election to the School Board shortly after she had taken up her new position gave her an extra insight into appalling conditions which were being ignored. She came to believe, with ever-growing conviction that, unless women had a say in the running of the country, the social situation could never be remedied. From experience she knew that, in the case of women's suffrage, the time for intellectual persuasion was over and, inspired by her daughter Christabel, who realised that the demand must now come from the poorer classes – the people themselves – she founded the Women's Social and Political Union.

Its growth was so rapid after the initial militant protest in 1905 that Mrs Pankhurst gradually found herself becoming so involved in speaking for the Union that she reluctantly gave up her official positions in order to devote her full energy to the cause.

Emmeline Pankhurst was an inspired and inspiring leader, a performer with the innate shyness of a great actress, a trait which some people misconstrued as aloofness. One of the WSPU organisers said, 'She was very, very human, so in touch with everything and her oratory was simply amazing. She had the sort of break in her voice that is the mark of a great orator.' Mrs Pankhurst was prepared to give up everything for the movement; she sacrificed her famil and her health in the ever optimistic hope that victory was at han The death of her son, Harry, in 1910, and of her sister, Mary Clark which followed rough treatment during a suffragette attack on Parliament in the same year, only served to encourage the grief-stricken Mrs Pankhurst to add to her programme of endless speaking-tours up and down the country. She sometimes had to face angry mobs who would shower her with rotten fruit and vegetables, but her witty repartee and magnetic platform presence was usually sufficient to overcome such attacks.

Mrs Pankhurst took upon herself the responsibility for all the militancy of WSPU members and was imprisoned thirteen times. Only one attempt was made to feed her by force, and on that occasion the mere sight of her standing in defiance to resist such an outrage compelled the prison officers to retreat with their equipment. In the final two years of the struggle (1913–14), Mrs Pankhurst, in a half-dying condition was continually in the limelight, desperately hoping that her actions and even her death might change the tide of affairs. She was indeed ready to die if necessary, but her conviction that she must see the fight through to the end seemed to endow her with a superhuman strength which she miraculously maintained to carry out her vital work in the war years that followed.

Mrs Pankhurst preached the WSPU gospel and put her name to every new policy, but it was in fact Christabel who initiated each move. Christabel Pankhurst was an unusually brilliant woman whose

Annie Kenney

Top left. Frederick Pethick Lawrence

Bottom left. Mrs Emmeline Pethick Lawrence

girlish, sometimes almost lethargic, appearance gave no indication of her highly intuitive intelligence and powerful command of all situations. She kept an eagle eye on the work of every organiser and speaker just as she closely followed government policy, and was usually able to anticipate the action of cabinet ministers with regard to suffragette affairs. Each week a leading article by Christabel appeared in the WSPU newspaper and her statements often seemed outrageous at the time of publication. However, the tactics she advocated were seldom ineffective and, though to many they were distasteful, they were certainly responsible for the continued success of the militant movement when every attempt had been made to suppress and destroy it. Christabel's belief in her own actions was so firm that she cared little what anyone thought of her.

Her younger sister Sylvia, on the other hand, had an entirely different approach to people. She was a true artist and as such was relatively unconcerned with the exclusively political side of the fight. Her sympathies lay with the under-privileged. She preferred to identify herself with them and to make actual contact with them rather than to devote herself to campaigning for their rights. Her clothes bore out her ideals, contrasting notably with the fashionable outfits worn by her mother and Christabel. Sylvia was also quite unable to reject, as they did, the help of former friends and acquaintances who belonged to the Independent Labour Party. Sylvia gained a tremendous following among the poorer classes, but those WSPU members who were seriously campaigning against the Government found her tiresome and over-emotional.

Mrs Flora Drummond

Without the devoted and untiring guidance of Frederick and Emmeline Pethick Lawrence, the movement could never have achieved the rapid success and financial stability that characterised its early days. The Pethick Lawrences were a childless couple and had spent their lives doing philanthropic work and furthering the cause of Socialism. Frederick Pethick Lawrence was brilliant, wealthy and although a qualified barrister, he did not practise but worked as editor of the *Labour Record and Review*. From 1906, when he was somewhat reluctantly drawn into the movement, until 1912, when the Pankhursts and Pethick Lawrences parted company, he was an invaluable adviser on policy; and, because of the mutual respect between him and Christabel, he was often able to temper her more extreme ideas. His great contribution to the WSPU was, however, his meticulous organisation of all their publicity. He had a passion for accuracy, and the highly professional printing of propaganda material and the WSPU newspaper, *Votes for Women*, was initiated and personally supervised by him at their headquarters.

Emmeline Pethick Lawrence came into the movement as honorary treasurer in 1906 and in this capacity her work was phenomenal. She was known as 'the most persuasive beggar in London' and, during the first five years of her work, she raised over £108,000 for WSPU funds. The secret of her success lay in her firm yet motherly influence over the local WSPU organisers, who were bound to ensure that every meeting and event for which they were responsible would pay for itself. Mrs Pethick Lawrence not only advised them on financial affairs but was also in constant correspondence with

Grace Roe

them, sending messages of encouragement and expressing the ideals of the WSPU in inspiring language. Although thoroughly practical in fulfilling her own responsibilities Mrs Pethick Lawrence was such an idealist that, when it came to the question of direct action on the battlefield, she was in some ways unrealistic. The actuality of her first imprisonment was such a shock to her that she was released before time with a breakdown. When she finally braved prison again and was forcibly fed, the effect upon her was so permanent that she never recovered. She did not possess the stoicism of the Pankhursts and firmly believed that the battle could be won without resorting to extreme measures. She felt that these would probably harm the suffragettes themselves as well as the people whose property they were attacking. She may have been right. In her own self-sacrificing way, she remained faithful to the WSPU until it became impossible, because of government demands upon her husband's finances, to stay with them any longer.

Free from the restraining Pethick Lawrence influence and yet still bearing their indelible mark, the WSPU embarked on the final period of violence.

Such were class distinctions at the beginning of the century that, in order to inspire working women to join the movement, it was necessary for other working women to convert them by their example. Annie Kenney, a mill girl from Oldham, became their champion and it was she who made the first militant protest with Christabel Pankhurst. Her honesty, warmth and good-humoured fervence with which she preached the WSPU policy won tremendous support. She was no intellectual and her methods of approaching those from whom she required assistance were child-like in the extreme. Yet people found her requests compelling and she always managed to draw to her women who could supply from behind the scenes the qualities she lacked. She succeeded in becoming chief organiser for the West of England and in running a flourishing campaign there from 1908 until 1912. However, as Mrs Pankhurst's chief organiser, which she became for a short period from March 1912 until her arrest in April 1913, Annie was out of her depth. With the leaders in prison, it was a difficult time. Position-seekers within the Union criticised her and somehow broke the spell – the strength that being a heroine had given her.

Flora Drummond, the other working-class woman who played such a prominent part in suffragette affairs, was impervious to criticism, She was a most colourful character, a little Scottish woman who, because of her dumpy appearance, became privately known as the 'Precocious Piglet'. This superseded her earlier nickname, 'Bluebell', after she had proved herself to be a match for any cabinet minister who refused to commit himself on the Votes for Woman issue. Winston Churchill was her particular target, and she would confront him and state the women's demands in a resounding voice whenever given the chance. She was a tireless worker and a great asset to the public relations of the Union, both through her encouragement to the rank and file and through her excellent *entente* with the Metropolitan Police Force.

The last great leader, who took over from Annie Kenney as Mrs Pankhurst's chief organiser, was Grace Roe. Because of her incredible loyalty, integrity and selflessness, Grace, in hiding, was able to keep the WSPU running when every conceivable attempt was being made to suppress it. As soon as she entered the office, offering herself as a worker in early 1909, Christabel realised that she was no ordinary person and she almost immediately appointed her as an organiser. Grace had a somewhat unconventional childhood and was, at an early age, encouraged by her mother to take an active interest in the affairs of the poor. Her family circle was a wide one and, in spite of her parents being advanced for the time and deeply interested in Socialism, Grace was brought up in Victorian style. This demanded the observation of etiquette and the knowledge of running a large household. When she was twelve years old, her mother died and Grace was sent away to one of the first co-educational boarding schools, where she excelled on the hockey field. Her upbringing thus prepared her for work as an organiser and her social training provided an ideal pattern for the ordering of group activities: she was able to manage a suffragette gathering with the same poise that she would have exercised at a family At Home.

She was, though, a natural leader and her authority was instantly recognised so that she was able to delegate work and bring out the best in everyone who came to help her, whatever their talents.

The scope and pressure of work within the WSPU was such that any woman who joined would automatically find her own level, and though no definitive distinction existed between members, there was a natural master–servant relationship. Those who were lazy or had other interests – such as men or religion – and those who failed to comply with the unwritten code, did not remain long within the organisation.

Women throughout the country were influenced by this new spirit of co-operation and enthusiastically joined the ranks, but it is difficult to understand why so many of them were willing to sacrifice their families and their health by submitting to imprisonment and forcible feeding. Such stoicism and suffering seems an excessive price to pay for the sake of the Parliamentary vote. Perhaps there was a subconscious reason for their action. When the war came in 1914, women were suddenly forced to take responsibility and to assume an entirely new position in society. In the crisis, many suffragettes took on key positions at home and their previous struggle for emancipation may well have been an inspired preparation to condition them to face the appalling event of war. Mrs Pankhurst seems to suggest this when calling on women to rally against the national enemy. She said, 'With that patriotism which has nerved women to endure torture in prison cells for the national good, we ardently desire that our country shall be victorious.'

The
New Women

The militant movement began as a Pankhurst family enterprise and, from 1903 until 1905, ticked over in Manchester with a mere handful of members, until the General Election of 1905 brought matters to a head. Christabel Pankhurst then made an outrageous intrusion (as it was regarded at the time) into the all-male world of politics. She suffered a token imprisonment for her audacity and from then on supporters of both sexes came flocking to the suffragette ranks.

Working-class people were the first to give open support to the suffragettes, but, within weeks of the initial protest, suffragists began to take more than a casual interest in the suffragettes. 'Ladies of rank' would be seen sitting unobtrusively at meetings alongside the rows of poor from the East End of London and, very soon, the impressive persistence of the leaders converted women from all walks of life to the militant cause.

They were wholeheartedly ready to try any new method which might speedily secure the privilege of political equality for which they had waited so long. They organised constitutional deputations to Parliament, they made daring individual calls on cabinet ministers, they paraded *en masse* in front of ministers' houses. But their questions met with evasive answers, their processions were roughly broken up and, to the horror of the well-bred ladies who took part, anyone who put up resistance was arrested.

Every true suffragette chose to become a martyr by going to prison rather than pay a token fine. The Home Office, quite unprepared to handle the phenomenon, felt that harsh treatment would put a speedy end to the problem of unruly women. The authorities condemned them to common criminal treatment but did not bargain for their extreme stoicism in the face of the appalling conditions and deprivations that such a sentence entailed. Instead of quelling the uprising, imprisonment only brought about new demonstrations and further imprisonments. Finally, the Government had to give in to a public demand that suffragettes be treated as political offenders.

On 13 October 1905, at a Liberal rally, Annie Kenney and Christabel Pankhurst were ignored when they questioned Churchill and Sir Edward Grey on women's suffrage. Finally they waved a banner and were arrested. They chose imprisonment rather than a fine, and achieved mass publicity. On her release Annie Kenney looks inspired and ingenuous: Christabel exhibits a youthful yet powerful self-assurance.

In the political field, they certainly made their mark by taking an active part in every by-election. Rarely did any Liberal candidate commit himself entirely to the cause of Votes for Women, and so the suffragettes would actively campaign against anyone who stood for that party and work up a fever of enthusiasm in his constituency to 'Keep the Liberal Out'. In many places their efforts completely changed the traditional voting pattern, particularly in the early years when political parties were unaware of what women's persuasive methods could accomplish. One of the suffragettes' renowned triumphs was the defeat of Winston Churchill as Liberal candidate for North West Manchester in 1908.

During the years from 1905 until 1908, the WSPU established itself as one of the wealthiest and best-run organisations in the country. Considering that, within eighteen months, there were branches established all over the British Isles, the ease with which the movement seemed to run itself was incredible. There was, in fact, an internal crisis among the WSPU leaders in 1907 when the Pankhursts and the Pethick Lawrences realised that, to prevent divergencies over policy, it was essential to run the movement on an autocratic rather than on a representational basis. Charlotte Despard and several followers who had held executive positions in the WSPU could not support the new conception and they resigned on the strength of their convictions.

Mrs Despard, a matriarchal figure and a spiritual leader rather than a soldier, then formed her own organisation, the Women's Freedom League. They pursued a policy of symbolic demonstration even going to the lengths of holding a ceremonial burial of the rejected women's enfranchisement bill on the plinth of Nelson's Column in Trafalgar Square. The WSPU had no time for such activities. Mrs Pankhurst announced after the split had occurred, 'We are not a school for teaching women how to use the vote, we are a militant movement and have got to get the vote next session.'

A TOPSY-TURVY DEMAND

The suffragettes followed up their first Manchester protest with one in London on 22 December 1905. The newly-elected Liberals, establishing 'the strongest ministry of modern times' at the Albert Hall, were questioned again on votes for women by Annie Kenney and Teresa Billington. They were hustled out and their display of an upside-down banner was seen as 'a topsy-turvy demand'.

17

Top left. By spring 1906 the militant movement was established and many working women had joined. Unsuccessful attempts to question ministers had achieved such publicity that the Prime Minister agreed to receive a mass deputation on 19 May. Supporters from all parts converged on London. Annie Kenney and Flora Drummond are welcoming a contingent from the north.

Bottom left. Several attempts to interview the Chancellor, Mr Asquith, a powerful opponent, led to the arrest of the 'ringleaders' in June 1906. Annie Kenney, Mrs Knight and Mrs Sparboro, all poor and harmless, are seen in front of WSPU Headquarters before their trial and six weeks' imprisonment. The WSPU named them 'Mr Asquith's Prisoners'.

Top right. WSPU offices were soon established at 4 Clement's Inn, although earlier meetings had been held at Pethick Lawrence's flat there. Here, in conference, are Flora Drummond, Christabel Pankhurst, Jessie Kenney (Annie's younger sister), Mrs Nellie Alma Martel (a former leader in the Australian women's suffrage movement), Mrs Pankhurst and Mrs Charlotte Despard.

Bottom right. The ranks of the WSPU steadily increased and so did the audacity of its timid working-women members. Many joined mass deputations to Parliament and if not arrested themselves, gave whole-hearted support to those who were. On 19 November 1906, Alice Milne, a Manchester suffragette, was welcomed on her release from prison by a banner-bearing contingent from Nine Elms.

Top left. By 1907 the WSPU had recruited a large number of full-time workers and organisers: well-dressed and well-spoken women of whom the press and public took notice. Here, a group of them attract attention as they wait outside the Houses of Parliament.

Bottom left. The first unpleasant confrontation with the police occurred when suffragette deputations to Parliament were refused audience with MPs. When Parliament opened on 13 February 1907, the suffragettes held their own women's parliament in the Caxton Hall and then marched with their 'resolutions' (rolled-up copies of their demands) to the House. The subsequent battle, in which they were turned back, resulted in over fifty arrests and imprisonments.

Above. The suffragettes who had been arrested bore no grudge against the police. Here the women are awaiting trial, in a prevailing atmosphere of good humour, although a certain nervousness is detectable. Among the prisoners are Irene Fenwick Miller, Teresa Billington, Adela and Christabel Pankhurst.

Mrs Charlotte Despard broke away from the WSPU to found the Women's Freedom League in October 1907. Her aim as president was to run the League on lines of representative government at the same time as fighting for the vote, and to educate women in the running of a true democracy.

Above. The women who joined Mrs Despard were idealists, believing in persuasive and symbolic methods of protest rather than in direct action. The picture was taken outside the Women's Freedom League headquarters in Adelphi, at the time of a summer bazaar. Surrounding Mrs Despard are Mrs Edith How Martyn, Marian Lawson and Teresa Billington Gregg.

Left. The suffragettes' newspaper and general source of information, *Votes for Women*, appeared in October 1907. Published under the expert direction of Pethick Lawrence, the cover of the early numbers displayed a cartoon by David Wilson, 'The Haunted House', showing a woman brooding over the Houses of Parliament.

Top left. Daily meetings were held to spread women's suffrage propaganda and draw in new recruits. Posters and handbills were printed for an important speaker, otherwise notice of meetings was chalked on pavements. 'Wait till I catch you bending' was a favourite remark directed at women chalkers.

Bottom left. The WSPU policy to 'Keep the Liberal Out' was vigorously pursued at every by-election. Mrs Pankhurst and her daughter Adela achieved astonishing success in reducing the Liberal majority at the numerous by-elections in which they campaigned in 1907 and 1908.

Top right. Hastings fishermen took a friendly, if amused, interest in the suffragettes who campaigned in the by-election of March 1908. Mrs Martel and Mrs Massey were photographed, chatting with the 'Admiral of the Fishing Fleet'. Earlier in the year, by contrast, Mrs Martel had been mobbed at Newton Abbot.

Bottom right. Suffragette tactics became more devious as the women realised the ineffectiveness of their direct approach to cabinet ministers. When the Cabinet Council met on 7 January 1908 to draft the King's speech, Mrs Drummond managed to enter the council chamber at 10 Downing Street by means of an elaborate ruse. Here her customary good humour yields to belligerent anger as she is arrested.

To coincide with the opening of Parliament in 1908, the suffragettes held a three-day women's parliament. On the third day, 13 February, Mrs Pankhurst, armed with a rolled 'resolution' and few lilies-of-the-valley, led a deputation to the Prime Minister. Soon after starting out she was arrested.

To Victory

Both success and failure marked the beginning of 1908. A women's suffrage bill was put forward and carried by a majority of 179 votes but, regarding its further progress, Asquith, the Prime Minister, pronounced that no electoral reform bill could be considered unless it had behind it the support of the women of the country. Certainly the suffragettes had won a tremendous following, but there were aspects of their fight – the deputations when women were handled by the police, the mass arrests and imprisonments – that disgusted and horrified some sections of the community. Every attempt to petition Parliament led to an increasing lack of decorum and loss of dignity.

The Pethick Lawrences, although they never actually spoke out against militancy, obviously preferred any method of peaceful demonstration to battlefield tactics. Mrs Pethick Lawrence, with her Salvation Army training, was continually devising new and colourful ways to advertise the movement. Pethick Lawrence's experience in journalism ensured that any publicity enterprise would be carried out in a thoroughly professional way. Their great triumph was the Hyde Park meeting of 21 June 1908 when some of the park railings had to be removed to accommodate the vast crowds, and the suffragettes provided London with a unique and unprecedented spectacle. Although the newspapers were filled with glowing accounts and the public was genuinely impressed, Asquith would only re-iterate his previous statement that support for the movement was insufficient to warrant any further parliamentary measures.

On hearing this, the militants again went into battle, now wearing their new purple, white and green uniform introduced at Hyde Park. Another mass march to Parliament resulted in many arrests. There was, for the first time real violence when two women decided to adopt the time-honoured method of window smashing, their objective being No 10, Downing Street. Although the leaders urged their followers not to take unauthorised action, when such an event did occur it was always condoned and thereafter established as yet another step in the progression of militancy.

During the summer of 1908, however, a theatrical type of demon-stration prevailed with women in fancy dress welcoming released prisoners and cars of triumphal martyrs being drawn round London by human horses. The general public enjoyed such scenes but were unprepared to give the women serious support.

Proof of this came in the autumn when, determined to put a speedy end to the fight, Mrs Pankhurst and Christabel invited the public to help 'rush the House of Commons'. This move caused a sensation and resulted in new arrests, a trial where two cabinet ministers were called as witnesses, and further imprisonments. Until Christmas when the Pankhursts were released, Londoners were constantly provided with the unusual diversion of women in prison costume parading the streets to protest about the imprison-ment of their leaders.

Top left. By the beginning of 1908 the suffragette leaders were considered sufficiently famous to occupy a place in Tussaud's Waxworks Exhibition. When Jean Tussaud sculpted Christabel he found her discussion 'quiet, most sensible and most intelligent'.

Bottom left. Hostile cabinet ministers proclaimed that there was no general support for the suffragette movement as there had been for previous franchise extensions. This challenge was taken up by Pethick Lawrence, who organised a phenomenal meeting on 21 June. Special trains brought supporters to London where 250,000 converged on Hyde Park.

Top right. Twenty waggons served as platforms for the 80 women speakers in the Park. Children and listeners were forced up on to the sides of Mrs Pankhurst's waggon by pressing crowds, while only she and (below her in the picture) the elderly suffrage pioneer, Mrs Wolstenholme Elmy, remained completly composed.

Bottom right. Despite glowing accounts of the Hyde Park meeting and overwhelming public appreciation, Asquith, now Prime Minister, refused to budge on the issue. A defiant deputation marched to Westminster on 30 June, and the first violence took place, two irate women throwing stones at the windows of 10 Downing Street.

Top left. Mrs Pethick Lawrence introduced uniforms and paraphernalia for the Hyde Park meeting which were then permanently adopted; the suffragette colours were worn every day and a new taste for pageantry developed. Prisoners of the 30 June deputation were each greeted appropriately on release. This tartan welcome is for Mary Phillips, a Scot.

Bottom left. Encouraged by public response to the Hyde Park meeting, the suffragettes called on the people to help them 'Rush the House of Commons' at the start of its autumn session. Christabel designed a handbill which the authorities found offensive.

Top right. On Sunday 11 October 1908, Mrs Pankhurst, Mrs Drummond and Christabel spoke from the plinth of Nelson's Column in Trafalgar Square, inviting the crowds to join the suffragettes' proposed assault on Parliament on 13 October. (Christabel is not in the picture.)

Bottom right. On 12 October, Mrs Pankhurst, Christabel and Mrs Drummond were summoned to appear at Bow Street police court. They defied the order having announced that they would surrender themselves at 6 o'clock the next evening. Mrs Pankhurst and Christabel spent the day hiding on the roof garden at Clement's Inn.

Top. Punctually at 6 pm on 13 October, Mrs Drummond, Mrs Pankhurst and Christabel arrived in the general office at Clement's Inn to surrender as they had promised. Inspector Jarvis read the warrant and they were then driven away to Bow Street police station.

Bottom. Before the 'Rush' on the House of Commons, the members of the deputation met at the Caxton Hall where Mrs Pethick Lawrence presided over a council of war, backed by Sylvia (in white dress). By this time, Mrs Pankhurst was at Bow Street.

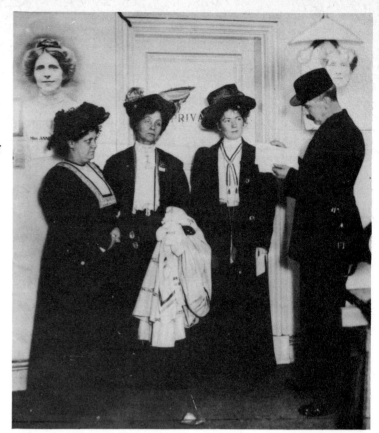

Top. The trial of the Suffragette leaders attracted much publicity. Lloyd George and Herbert Gladstone were among witnesses for the defence. The drawn-out case was eventually cut short when the magistrate, dismissing political reasons for the protest, sentenced the older leaders to three months' imprisonment and Christabel to ten weeks.

Bottom. Officially political prisoners, the leaders still had to wear prison clothing and maintain silence. Wearied by these restrictions, Mrs Pankhurst and Christabel led a mutiny on 1 November during the exercise period. They linked arms and talked while spontaneous cheers brought wardresses running to herd women back to cells.

Top left. When Mrs Drummond was released because of pregnancy, she openly deplored the prison treatment of her colleagues. At her suggestion, workers and organisers dressed in mock prison garb and paraded the London streets. Led by Florence Haig and supervised by Jessie Kenney, they left Clement's Inn to march to Holloway.

Top right. Elaborate celebrations awaited the leaders on their release from Holloway, and the Home Secretary, in anticipation of the rejoicings, ordered the release of Mrs Pankhurst and Christabel earlier than announced. Turned out late on Saturday evening 19 December, they were welcomed by only a few followers.

Bottom. Despite government efforts to suppress all celebrations, Mrs Pankhurst and Christabel rode through the West End of London on Saturday 22 December in a triumphal carriage drawn by white horses. Bands played 'See the Conquering Hero Comes'.

By 1909, women's suffrage was the one subject mentioned in the newspapers every day. The cause had been taken up by societies all over the country, cashing-in on the success of suffragette propaganda and imitating suffragette methods of organisation. As a result their aim was no longer a solely political one, but also one of demonstrating the capabilities of women. The suffragettes saw danger in this general enthusiasm; they might lose recruits who wavered over the ethics of militancy. But it was soon quite apparent, as warfare was speedily stepped up during 1909, that only a certain type of woman, resolute and uncompromising, was anyway suitable to carry out suffragette activities.

The suffragettes' largest assault yet on the Houses of Parliament was followed by a window-smashing raid on government offices, and the subsequent imprisonments resulted in hunger striking and release before time of all the women concerned. The suffragettes had once more been deprived of political prisoner rights and it was because of this that they rebelled, suffered the indignity and filth of punishment cells and finally decided to starve. It was an ordeal that required tremendous strength and willpower and one to which sheltered middle-class women might seem unequal. However, the suffragettes' complete devotion to their cause did not, in theory, admit any thought of self and they were literally prepared to die if need be.

These tribulations and their own internal struggles they kept to themselves and, to all outward appearances, the day-to-day militant action of the suffragettes was mainly light-hearted. Despite its innocuous levity, many people nevertheless found it very irritating. Because of their interruptions at political meetings, women were now banned from attending them and their ruses to gain the attention of cabinet ministers became ever more complex. Suffragettes would conceal themselves in halls where MPs were speaking and suddenly interrupt the meeting from under the platform. Disguises were often used and any harmless way of allowing a minister to hear 'votes for women' pleaded was considered fair game.

On the other hand, personal affront to the Prime Minister was going too far and, after he had twice been waylaid on holiday, security measures for all leading ministers were tightened. The attitude of the general public was also beginning to change. In several towns suffragettes had been mobbed for opposing Liberal ministers, but elsewhere the crowds had sided with them in protest outside halls where ministers were speaking.

In September, barricades against such disturbances were put up in Birmingham where Asquith was to speak. Defiant suffragettes showered down ginger-beer bottles from the roofs of surrounding buildings, and it was after this particular action that militancy and its results took on a far more sinister aspect. Dangerous stone-throwers could not be allowed to remain at large if they gained release through hunger strike, and the authorities felt that forcible feeding was the only method by which they could keep the women in prison. Their adoption of this practice raised an outcry, not least among the militants themselves who now felt only bitterness towards those ministers who had failed to recognise all their peaceful attempts. It was a very dangerous situation where many suffragettes were prepared to go further than their leaders wished.

Fortunately, at crisis point, the likelihood of a general election made a timely excuse for a temporary halt to militant action. However, the suffragettes remained in the forefront of the news through the exploits of Lady Constance Lytton. Outraged by the class discrimination in the treatment of prisoners, Lady Constance dis-

Heroines and Martyrs

guised herself as a poor working woman and threw a stone at a minister's car When previously imprisoned as a titled lady her treatment had been preferential and, after scrupulous medical tests, she was released before time because of her weak heart. Now, no test was made, she was forcibly fed and when she finally broke down and her identity was discovered, her health was ruined and she became a permanent invalid. Herbert Gladstone, the Home Secretary, was severely criticised and on the return to Parliament of a Liberal government, was 'promoted' to the governorship of South Africa. Nothing could be done about Lady Constance's case and the new Home Secretary, Winston Churchill, although an old friend of Lady Constance's brother, was thoroughly opposed to the suffragettes and ruthless in refusing to make concessions.

The gaiety and spontaneity that marked the earlier days of the movement was at an end as the suffragettes became ever more weighed down with responsibilities endangering their own lives.

The post card was produced by the Suffrage Atelier to publicise Tax Resistance, one of the earliest forms of protest. Women's suffrage enthusiasts who felt that they could make an active contribution to the cause joined independent groups; artists formed a league as early as 1907, actresses in 1909.

Top right. By 1909 the movement had become so concentrated on London that in Manchester there was a marked apathy among workers and organisers. So Mrs Pankhurst and Christabel made a special tour of the area. Christabel's meeting on 15 January was announced by 'human advertisement' because wet weather had prevented chalking parties.

Bottom right. Suffragettes were sent in advance of a by-election to establish temporary headquarters and prepare local inhabitants for the arrival of WSPU speakers. Hundreds of meetings took place in the days before the poll. Here, Theresa Garnett, Nellie Crocker, Gladys Roberts and Edith New are seen at Hawick in February 1909.

WOMENS SUFFRAGE REFORM

NO TAXATION WITHOUT REPRESENTATION

VOTES FOR WOMEN
DEPUTATION
HOUSE OF
COMMONS
WEDNESDAY
TO THE RIGHT HON
H. H.
ASQUITH

Left. A suffragette deputation was planned for 24 February 1909, and to publicise the event they took advantage of a post-office innovation, 'The Human Letter', price three-pence. Elspeth McLelland and Daisy Soloman were officially addressed and conveyed by special messenger to 10 Downing Street. They were rejected and returned.

Top. Mrs Pethick Lawrence was arrested after leading the 4 February deputation. On 16 April her triumphal return to headquarters was led by a symbolic Joan of Arc, followed by a procession of women and children with flowers. Elsie Howey, a clergyman's daughter, represented the newly canonised saint, Mrs Lawrence's heroine.

Bottom. While Mrs Lawrence was in prison, WSPU members subscribed to buy her a new car, an Austin, painted and upholstered in the suffragette colours; Vera Holme (ex-d'Oyly Carte) became its uniformed chauffeur. Here, suffragette speakers, Ada Flatman and Georgina Brackenbury, are being conveyed to a meeting.

The National Women's Social & Political Union

4, Clement's Inn,
London.

The Women's Exhibition 1909

Prince's Skating Rink
Knightsbridge **London**

May 13th to 26th

Programme
Price 3ᴰ

The Woman's Press,
4, Clement's Inn, London, W.C.

Left. The Women's Exhibition was initially a fund-raising bazaar. It was also an attempt to publicise the peaceful and constructive side of the militant movement. Sylvia Pankhurst painted allegorical murals for the main exhibition hall and also designed the trumpeting angel on the programme.

Top. The suffragettes discovered that the 1869 Bill of Rights entitled subjects to petition Parliament. Quoting this statute they embarked on their deputation of 29 June, sending Vera Holme in advance as a herald. Mounted, she was immune to arrest, but police stopped her and blocked her approach to Parliament.

Bottom. The Bill of Rights deputation, made up of a group of highly distinguished women, was refused audience. Other women then attempted an assault on the House and some smashed windows of government offices. 108 were arrested. Women awaiting trial in the police-court yard next day baffled police identification by their elegant appearance.

THE SCENE OF THE SUFFRAGETTES' MARTYRDOM:
~ IN HOLLOWAY PRISON ~

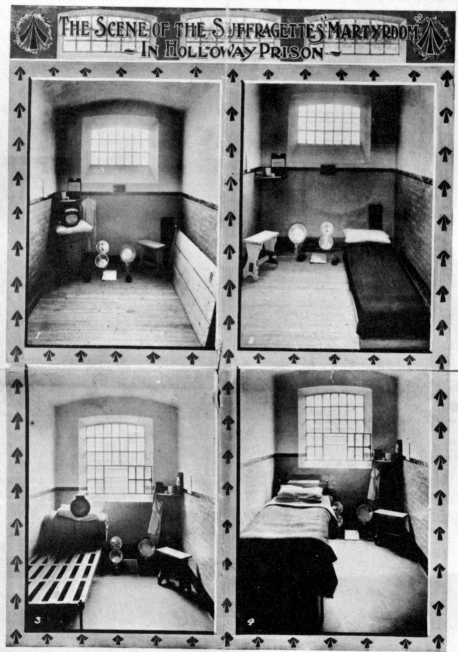

1. A PRISON CELL, SIMILAR TO THOSE OCCUPIED BY THE SUFFRAGETTES, AS IT IS IN THE DAYTIME, WITH THE PLANK-BED AGAINST THE WALL AND THE BEDDING FOLDED UP.

2. A PRISON CELL, SIMILAR TO THOSE OCCUPIED BY THE SUFFRAGETTES, AS IT IS AT NIGHT-TIME, WITH THE PLANK-BED AND THE BEDDING IN PLACE.

3. A PRISON CELL FOR CONSUMPTIVES, WITH A WINDOW THAT IS LARGER THAN THAT OF THE ORDINARY CELL, SHOWING THE BED AND THE BEDDING AS THEY ARE IN THE DAYTIME.

4. A PRISON CELL FOR CONSUMPTIVES, WITH A WINDOW THAT IS LARGER THAN THAT OF THE ORDINARY CELL, SHOWING THE BED AND THE BEDDING AS THEY ARE AT NIGHT.

Holloway Prison has been very much in the public eye since it became the scene of the militant Suffragettes' "martyrdom." It is particularly to the fore at the moment, owing to Mr. Herbert Gladstone's visit to it after Suffragettes' complaints, the statements of wardresses that the Suffragettes are the most unruly prisoners with whom they have to deal, and the serving of summonses on two of the militant ladies for alleged assault on wardresses while in Holloway Prison.

PHOTOGRAPHS SPECIALLY TAKEN FOR "THE ILLUSTRATED LONDON NEWS" BY BULLOCK.

Above. Hunger-striking suffragettes acquired strength through passionate loyalty to their cause and Christabel, aware of this, obtained access to a window outside which overlooked the suffragettes' cells, and waved to her supporters. In response they dangled WSPU scarves and ties from the prison windows which they had defiantly broken.

Left. It was agreed in court that the suffragettes' right to petition was justified, and only the fourteen stone-throwers of 29 June were prosecuted. Imprisoned in Holloway, they were refused political rights and in protest they adopted the hunger strike. Their 'martyrdom' attracted widespread publicity.

Top. Women were banned from Liberal meetings in 1909, but they entered halls by trickery and made their presence felt. Mrs Bessie Newsam, in her husband's clothes, successfully joined the audience at the Dome in Brighton on 4 January 1910, and questioned Asquith.

Bottom. Unmarried, Lady Constance Lytton had devoted her life to social causes; she committed herself to the suffragettes by joining the deputation of February 1909, and was imprisoned. She knew her title was an asset to the movement but was distressed when, because of it, she received preferential treatment in prison.

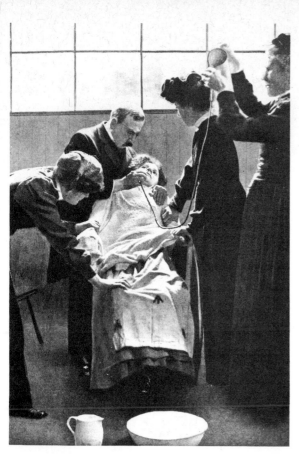

Top. Suffragettes on hunger strike necessarily had to be released from prison before their sentences had expired, but following an attack on a car in which the Prime Minister was travelling in September 1909, the prison authorities decided forcibly to feed women who had used violence.

Bottom. Hoping that the militancy of an Earl's daughter would carry weight, Lady Constance Lytton volunteered for a stone-throwing protest, at Newcastle in October 1909. Lloyd George's car was her target, but she mistakenly stoned Sir Walter Runciman's. She was escorted to the police station by detectives, with crowds following.

Calm Before the Storm

Militancy had reached a dangerous stage by the beginning of 1910. A truce had been called while the General Election was in progress and, to the great relief of most of the active suffragettes, it was afterwards prolonged. They were exhausted after the intensive and taxing campaigns of 1909 and they welcomed a peaceful period. But it was not one of rest for, after the Lady Constance Lytton episode, Lord Lytton, her brother, now himself passionately involved in the cause, organised a group of MPs to form a Conciliation Committee. The bill which they drafted and put forward on behalf of women's suffrage was a compromise, but if successful it was thought that it would prove to be the thin end of the wedge. It was welcomed by both suffragists and suffragettes – only the far-seeing Christabel Pankhurst was sceptical – and now all campaigning activities were directed towards promoting the bill.

During this very tense period, the suffragettes were optimistic. In June, they staged a huge demonstration and procession immaculately planned in which many other suffrage societies joined, believing that at last the fight was nearly won. But, shortly afterwards, when a suffrage deputation was received by Asquith, he stressed the fact that, although the conciliation bill had so far been successful in Parliament, certain cabinet ministers were opposed to it, and he implied that he held little hope for its future.

Many suffragettes wished to resume militancy immediately but their leaders, aware that a far fiercer type of warfare would have to be adopted if the truce were broken, prevailed on their followers to keep the peace until every persuasive method had been tried. In spite of the phenomenal propaganda on behalf of the conciliation bill and the continual lobbying of MPs who had pledged their support, its prospects began to fade as leading cabinet ministers, including Churchill and Lloyd George, spoke forcibly against it on its second reading. Again there was a majority of votes in favour of the bill, but when it came to the ballot on its further progress, those who had been faithfully pledged to it now abandoned their support and it

The general election of 1910 brought an opportune halt in militancy. All suffragette efforts were concentrated on campaigning against the Liberals, in particular the Prime Minister. Hundreds of WSPU posters and post cards were printed showing 'Double-face Asquith' who was proposing reforming the House of Lords.

THE RIGHT DISHONOURABLE DOUBLE-FACE ASQUITH.

VOTES FOR WOMEN

Women's Social and Political Union.

4, Clement's Inn, London, W.C.

Citizen Asq—th: " Down with privilege of birth—up with Democratic rule ! "

Monseigneur Asq—th: " The rights of government belong to the aristocrats by birth—men. No liberty or equality for women ! "

was placed with other parliamentary business to be taken up when time permitted.

Still the suffragettes held their truce until they saw, at the beginning of the autumn parliamentary session, that there was about to be a further general election and that negotiations over their bill, which had gone so far would have to begin all over again under a re-elected parliament, they took the constitutional upheaval as directed against them personally. They failed to see the true reason for the dissolution, they felt betrayed, and their one idea was to get some sort of assurance from the existing government while it was still possible to do so.

Their march to Parliament and disastrous confrontation with the police took place on a November afternoon which afterwards became known as Black Friday. Winston Churchill, the Home Secretary, had issued strict orders to the police with the object of avoiding arrests. He had not bargained with the women's strenuous persistence and the police, in their efforts to turn back the suffragettes, became so vindictive that women were bruised, battered and assaulted. Two died and many others were permanently injured. Nearly two hundred women were arrested after this deputation and another four days later but, on Churchill's orders, the majority were discharged without trial.

Suffragists, and Lord Lytton in particular, strongly disapproved of the latest Suffragette action. They still held hopes for the fated conciliation bill. 1911 was Coronation Year and even the suffragettes felt that militancy would be improper while London was fêting the new king and queen. Crisis point was finally reached at the end of that November when Asquith unexpectedly proposed a general electoral reform bill which would enfranchise the men of the country who were still voteless but which would completely obviate the conciliation bill.

The suffragettes, now armed with stones and led in Mrs Pankhurst's absence by Mrs Pethick Lawrence, set out for Parliament and, when turned back, dispatched their missiles through the windows of government offices and shops all along Whitehall and the Strand.

Above. In Newcastle, Lady Constance Lytton was preferentially released. Resolving to expose the authorities' discrimination she disguised herself as 'Jane Warton, spinster and seamstress', and threw another stone on 14 January. Previously her heart had always been tested but now she was forcibly fed without examination and her latent condition developed into paralysis.

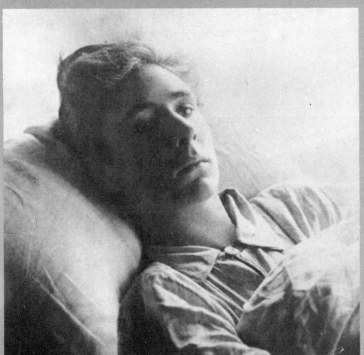

Left. Harry, Mrs Pankhurst's youngest child, was a faithful supporter of the WSPU. He finally chose a farming career but soon contracted polio. To raise funds for his treatment, Mrs Pankhurst lectured in America but on her return Harry was completely paralysed and he died on 5 January 1910, aged twenty.

Top. It looks as though suffragettes, tearing down Kingsway in a horse-drawn fire engine, were performing some battle manoeuvre. But at this time, March 1910, a truce was on. The women were optimistic about the proposed Conciliation Bill and were merely advertising an Albert Hall meeting.

Bottom. Despite Cabinet opposition, the Conciliation Bill passed through its preliminary stages but a constitutional crisis, demanding another election, threatened the bill. The suffragettes, intent on securing its future, again met in the Caxton Hall on 18 November (later called 'Black Friday') before sending a deputation of distinguished women to Parliament.

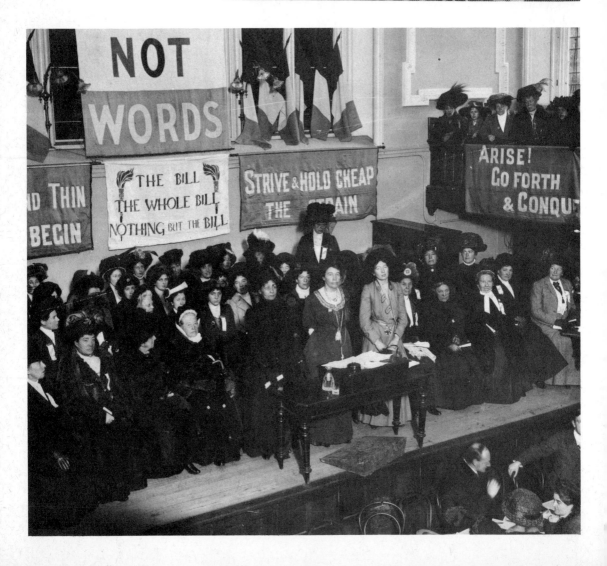

Top. On 'Black Friday' Churchill, the Home Secretary, instructed the police to drive away the women rather than arrest them. Unable to combat fierce suffragette resistance outside the House, the police reacted with brutality. Many press photographs were suppressed and only those showing the women as aggressors were printed.

Bottom. The Conciliation Bill still held good under the new 1911 Liberal Government and the suffragettes resumed their truce. They welcomed a Women's Freedom League proposal for a non-militant census protest, and on the night of 2 April hundreds of women spent the night camping out to avoid the count.

WOMAN'S PRESS, COLOURS & TEA DEPT.

Top left. In 1911, Coronation Year, peaceful propaganda flourished. The work of sympathetic artists, playwrights and politicians was published by the WSPU and sold at the Woman's Press, their shop at 156 Charing Cross Road. The picture shows the press cart which distributed 'Votes for Women'.

Bottom left. Besides literature, the Woman's Press stocked items specially made in the suffragette colours: ribbons, shantung motor scarves, pencils, playing cards and even cigarettes; also 24-piece tea sets, packets of 'Votes for Women' tea and boxes of stationery, all embellished with designs by Sylvia.

Top right. A meeting with Mrs Pankhurst made Dr Ethel Smyth, the musician, decide to dedicate two years of her life to the suffragettes. Her marching song, heard for the first time in January 1911, became the WSPU anthem. Dr Ethel once conducted it in Holloway with a toothbrush while the women prisoners sang.

Bottom right. Yoshio Markino, the Japanese artist, caught the spirit of the Albert Hall meeting of 23 March 1911. Christabel (centre) and Mrs Pankhurst (left) defiantly forecast serious consequences if the Conciliation Bill was rejected. Dr Ethel Smyth, in academic dress, conducted the choir (above) in the 'March of the Women'.

At the Albert Hall

51

SUFFRAGETTE PROCESSION JUNE 17, 1911.

Top left. 'At Homes' helped to recruit new members and to increase WSPU funds which, by summer 1911, had reached a £100,000 target. Here, at Rockstone House, Pinner, Lady Constance Lytton addressed Mrs Terrero's 140 guests and afterwards received a presentation from the children of Ambrose Heal, the progressive London furnisher.

Above. The coronation procession did not pass entirely without a militant warning. Mrs Saul Soloman, wife of a former governor of Cape Colony, who had taken a prominent part on Black Friday, was still in a wheel chair following her injuries. In spite of prevailing cheerfulness, her banner struck an ominous note.

Bottom left. A march of suffrage societies, 40,000 strong, took place on 17 June 1911, five days before the Coronation. An elaborate display of pageantry demonstrated both national and international support. The 700 suffragette ex-prisoners, under Laurence Houseman's famous banner, carried lances with shimmering silver pennants in the colours.

Broken Windows

Mass window smashing by the suffragettes shocked the country, but so did Asquith's attitude in substituting a manhood suffrage bill for the conciliation bill. In addition, he made it clear that in his opinion votes for women would be a disastrous mistake. The public did not outrightly condemn the militants, as might have been expected, for they saw justification in the protest and felt that there must have been extreme provocation to induce the high-minded and peace-loving Mrs Pethick Lawrence to lead it.

The suffragettes justified their action after the incident while they were preparing for a further demonstration. They proclaimed stone throwing as a time-honoured political argument and cited the Franchise Riots before the 1832 Reform Bill when Nottingham Castle was burned and half the city of Bristol was destroyed. Although Mrs Pankhurst repeatedly asked Asquith to give her an interview he refused to see her, and so the suffragettes, as they had threatened, pursued the argument with the stone. Their first attack, led by Mrs Pankhurst, took place four days before the one they had advertised. The manoeuvre was minutely timed and planned so that every window of every shop on one side of the main shopping streets of the West End of London was simultaneously smashed.

Without delay the WSPU offices were raided, Mrs Pankhurst and the Pethick Lawrences were arrested and Christabel would certainly have been taken too, had she not managed to disappear. Her escape caused more sensation than all the militancy. She was a popular figure and commercial enterprises quickly cashed in on her disappearance for advertising purposes and as a subject for new games. It was thought that Christabel had not gone far, for explanations of policy in pamphlet form signed by her, as well as her leading article in *Votes for Women* – unsigned but unmistakable – continued to appear. After the raid on the offices and despite the leaders' absence, the official work of the Union continued as though nothing had happened. The system had been so well organised that for several months it seemed to be continuing under its own impetus.

In fact Christabel had escaped to France, but this was not made public for six months and in the meantime Annie Kenney had secretly been made Chief Organiser. Having been organiser for the West Country since 1908 she was not an object of suspicion and was able to travel freely and frequently between London and Paris to report on activities at home and to receive instructions for the future. In spite of her enthusiasm, Annie's personal leadership was not strong enough to combat powerful intellectual personalities who began to take official WSPU business into their own hands. The office staff, receiving two sets of directions, started to become very slack and in the provinces, too, the organisers lacked purpose.

It was at this point that Grace Roe began to show her remarkable powers of leadership. At a local by-election, she had realised that the work of the assembled suffragette contingent was less than ineffective. She assumed authority, separated the antagonistic elements and, at the eleventh hour, ensured that the suffragettes' campaign was effective. From this time onwards, Grace gradually took over command at Christabel's instigation so that when Annie Kenney was finally arrested a year later, Grace was completely ready to step into her place.

As most of the active militants were imprisoned after the stone throwing, there was a lull in suffragette performance so far as the general public was concerned. Within prison, on the other hand, the women continued to prove a source of outrage and confusion. For a time, the prison treatment of suffragettes had been very moderate with all concessions granted, but now, probably because of the

In November 1911, Asquith replaced
the Conciliation Bill with a measure
to enfranchise the last of the male
population. Furious that their bill
was 'torpedoed', the suffragettes
smashed windows in protest, and
they renewed their attack on property in March 1912, with an
onslaught on West End shops.

vast numbers to be accommodated, all militants, including the leaders, were denied full political prisoner treatment. Discontent was already stirring when the leaders – including Pethick Lawrence who had never joined a militant assault – were all sentenced to nine months in the Second Division. Because of the pressure of worldwide protest, the leaders were eventually transferred to the First Division, but the status of other suffragette prisoners remained unchanged.

Universal hunger strike was followed by a ghastly series of forcible feeding operations and one woman threw herself over the prison staircase in a suicide attempt. Both Pethick Lawrences were forcibly fed but Mrs Pankhurst defied the doctors to touch her. In Parliament, George Lansbury, the Socialist pioneer, denounced Asquith as 'a torturer of innocent women' and was ordered to leave the House.

All this gave rise to a new outbreak of militancy. Window smashing began again, and in July 1912 the first serious arson attempt was discovered. On Asquith's visit to Dublin later in the month, a hatchet was thrown into his carriage. On the other hand, suffragettes who interrupted a speech by Lloyd George in Wales were stripped naked by hostile crowds.

Soon after the leaders were released from prison they left the country. Mrs Pankhurst went to Christabel in Paris and the Pethick Lawrences to Canada, expecting to mount a new campaign on their return in the autumn. Pethick Lawrence was being held responsible

While newspaper boys announced the 'suffragette fiasco', police were obliged to guard the windows of West End shops smashed by suffragette hammers. After the failure of their constitutional deputations, culminating in the Black Friday brutalities, the women maintained that plate glass was a more suitable sacrifice than human life.

for costs after the window smashing, and while he was away bailiffs took charge of his Surrey home. But a far greater shock awaited the Pethick Lawrences on their return. The Pankhursts had decided that they must now pursue a policy of militancy of which they knew the Pethick Lawrences would disapprove; their decision resulted in a split in the leadership. Henceforward 'Peths' and 'Panks' would go their separate ways. The younger women, those who wanted excitement and were prepared for danger, remained in the WSPU. Some women left the movement altogether at this stage, while the intellectuals and those who wished to continue campaigning but who could not condone further violence joined the Pethick Lawrences. The Pethick Lawrences continued to produce *Votes for Women* and carry on a persuasive campaign while Christabel inaugurated a new weekly paper, *The Suffragette*, which was unguarded in content but which never quite overstepped the mark of propriety.

Mrs Pankhurst, strangely alone on the Albert Hall platform, opened the autumn campaign with an incitement to violence. But before a full-scale militant outbreak one last hope remained that influence of a constitutional nature might change circumstances. George Lansbury resigned his seat as Member for Bow and Bromley, and stood for re-election on the votes for women issue. The East End women wholeheartedly supported him, but the male electorate, tired of being brainwashed from all sides by suffragettes of every denomination, voted against him. It was a bitter disappointment but still peaceful persuasion was tried. Out of the Bow and Bromley campaign another scheme developed.

The suffragettes had discovered that working women could express their plight in moving terms and it was thought that if a deputation representing different trades were to call on the two ministers who were professing to be in favour of a women's suffrage amendment to Asquith's manhood suffrage bill, they might add weight to those ministers' intentions. Working women from all over the country assembled in London only to be rebuffed when it was announced in Parliament that the manhood suffrage bill was withdrawn.

Full-scale warfare began. Windows were smashed, pillar-boxes fired, telegraph wires were cut and golf greens destroyed. The outrage which finally caused Mrs Pankhurst's condemnation to three years' imprisonment was the bombing of the new house under construction for Lloyd George near the golf course at Walton Heath.

Further cases of arson followed but the suffragettes had a strictly limited range of targets. Not even a cat or canary must be harmed. Arson took place in the early hours and only empty premises – sports pavilions, stations, vacant houses and churches – were burnt down. Annie Kenney was arrested soon after Mrs Pankhurst's trial when she unashamedly proclaimed that the WSPU policy of attack on property would continue; and when the Union demonstrated its strength at an Albert Hall meeting where £15,000 was raised. A government raid on the WSPU offices inevitably followed. The office staff were arrested, all papers were confiscated and facilities for printing *The Suffragette* were removed.

As chief organiser, Grace Roe, who had managed to elude the police, gathered together all the workers still available and organised an amazing coup whereby *The Suffragette*, due to appear on the following day, was miraculously printed and ready on time for distribution, bearing on the cover the one word 'RAIDED'. After this, Grace Roe immediately adopted a disguise which she was obliged to change several times during the following months, and she travelled directly to Paris to discuss with Christabel the future of the Union.

On 1 March, Mrs Pankhurst was arrested after the window-smashing raid and on 5 March, following a further outbreak, police raided Clement's Inn and took the Pethick Lawrences. Christabel escaped and her absence caused national speculation. The Flashograph Company printed an optical toy to celebrate her disappearance.

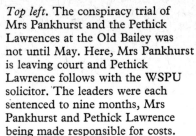

Top left. The conspiracy trial of Mrs Pankhurst and the Pethick Lawrences at the Old Bailey was not until May. Here, Mrs Pankhurst is leaving court and Pethick Lawrence follows with the WSPU solicitor. The leaders were each sentenced to nine months, Mrs Pankhurst and Pethick Lawrence being made responsible for costs.

Bottom left. As the press discovered, in September 1912 Christabel had escaped to France. Immune to arrest she continued to direct the affairs of the WSPU from a flat in Paris. Suffragette messengers secretly carried dispatches between her and the anonymous organisers in London.

Top right. Following Mrs Pankhurst's strong incitement to militancy in February 1913, Lloyd George's house was bombed. Mrs Pankhurst was sentenced to three years. Militancy increased and on 30 April suffragette headquarters at Lincoln's Inn were raided. Here, an emergency copy of the WSPU paper is being composed at the Daily Herald Offices.

Bottom right. Police raiding WSPU headquarters arrested suspect staff and tried to prevent the printing of *The Suffragette*. Grace Roe, secretly appointed chief organiser on Annie Kenney's arrest two weeks before, eluded detectives, procured emergency funds and before leaving for Paris arranged for the appearance next day of the dramatic-looking newspaper.

The
Suffragette

EDITED BY CHRISTABEL PANKHURST
The Official Organ of the Women's Social and Political Union.
Price 1d. Weekly (......)

FRIDAY, MAY 2, 1913.

No. 29. VOL. I.

RAIDED!!

Despite heavy sentences, militant suffragettes secured early release by hunger striking, but their bitterness towards the government increased and with it their militancy. The Pankhursts and Pethick Lawrences separated over this issue in Autumn 1912 and soon afterwards a concerted attack started on pillar boxes.

Renewed suffragette violence followed the leaders' premature release on 24 June 1912. It reached culmination in Dublin in July when a hatchet was thrown into the carriage in which Asquith was travelling. To protect the suffragette image, Mary Phillips greeted the returning Asquith in Chester with a bag of flour.

Top left. The 'conspirators', the office staff who had been arrested on 30 April, appeared at Bow Street for a preliminary hearing on the next day. Outside the court, triumphant suffragette paper sellers displayed copies of the 'RAIDED' issue.

Bottom left. News of the leaders' long sentences and subsequent unfair treatment in prison caused universal outcry. Mass forcible feeding followed a hunger-striking protest and both Pethick Lawrences were victims. The Labour pioneer, George Lansbury (speaking here in Hyde Park), denounced Asquith in Parliament as 'a torturer of innocent women'.

Top. Mrs Pankhurst exhorted: 'There is something that governments care far more for than human life and that is the security of property and so it is through property that we shall strike the enemy. Be militant each in your own way.' The picture shows a response by the crippled May Billinghurst.

Bottom. The last peaceful attempts to reintroduce women's suffrage to the Parliamentary agenda failed. Lansbury's stand for the suffragettes was unsuccessful, as was a working women's deputation to Lloyd George, a professed supporter. Arson followed the rebuffs, empty buildings were gutted and the picture shows the wreck of Saunderton station.

Twenty-four hours after the raid on the WSPU headquarters their flag was again flying over the building. *The Suffragette*, which the Government had tried to suppress, was openly sold outside the court where the trials of the office staff were taking place, and there were public outcries and demonstrations against the suppression of freedom of the press and of free speech.

Another Government measure against which there was nationwide protest was the introduction of a Prisoners Temporary Discharge for Ill-health Bill – a measure to prevent the unconditional release of suffragette prisoners after hunger strike. It was termed by Pethick Lawrence the 'Cat and Mouse Act'. Under its conditions, a prisoner was released when dangerously weak from starvation, confined to a closely guarded house of her own choosing and, after a prescribed period, was then expected to have recovered sufficiently to return to prison.

The Home Secretary, Reginald McKenna, introduced the Act after some alarming cases had resulted from forcible feeding and because of a general outcry over the adoption of this practice. Arson and the threat of bombs were terrorising the public and many people favoured the idea of allowing the suffragettes to starve to death or, alternatively, deporting them. Mrs Pankhurst was the first victim of the 'Cat and Mouse Act', and it looked as though her three-year sentence would be interminable since she firmly persisted in hunger striking and later in thirst striking. This action so much weakened her already damaged health that within two days she was at the point of death and had to be released. Her convalescence lasted longer than the allocated time, and she felt so degraded and frustrated by the constant guard of detectives surrounding the house where she was staying, that her recovery was impeded by sheer mental anguish. Already sections of the public were condemning the 'Cat and Mouse Act' as just another form of torture and saying, 'Let Mrs Pankhurst die!'

An undercurrent of despair ran through the suffragette ranks at the plight of their leader. To show this, however, would have been contrary to all their principles and, although their policy of damage to property in no way slackened, they were, at the same time, able to produce the most feminine and civilised summer fete and fair at the Empress Rooms.

Emily Wilding Davison was a brilliant graduate, a former teacher and a devoted WSPU worker. She was already in her early forties and had believed for some time that one martyr could save the cause. On previous occasions when suffragette affairs were critical, she had attempted in dramatic circumstances to take her life. Now at last she achieved her aim when she met her death on the Epsom Racecourse. It was Derby Day, 1913, and she had tried during the great race to stop the King's horse by hurling herself in front of it. The coup caused a public sensation, but only under extreme difficulty were the suffragettes able to exploit the event. All known suffragettes were in danger of arrest and Grace Roe, secretly leading the movement, was restricted by being disguised as a chorus girl. Nevertheless, she organised a funeral procession which left an unforgettable impression on all who saw it. Just as an emaciated Mrs Pankhurst, still on licence, was about to step into the carriage in which she was to ride in the procession, detectives intervened and re-arrested her, taking her back to prison for the duration of the funeral. Her carriage was dramatically driven empty in the procession and, somewhat surprisingly, the Government's action was universally condemned as being in bad taste.

Defiance of the intolerable 'Cat and Mouse Act' now became the

Death for the Cause

suffragettes' chief concern. By means of elaborate ruses and the co-operation of friends many 'mice' on licence were escaping from the houses where they were guarded. Several women, when they had freed themselves, immediately committed further outrages. The Act was proving totally ineffective as every day militant strategy became more ingenious. Mrs Pankhurst and Annie Kenney were now smuggled out of captivity and brought to speak at weekly meetings at the London Pavilion. Disguises were used and often as many as a hundred women would be involved in staging the escape. The Pavilion meetings were charged with emotion as Mrs Pankhurst and Annie Kenney appeared, newly released from prison, and sometimes so ill that Mrs Pankhurst was even wheeled on to the stage in an invalid chair.

The duration of 'Cat and Mouse' licences was rarely longer than a fortnight but, since the leaders were often unfit to return to prison when their licences expired, they were still at large to make a public appearance if it could be manoeuvred. They knew for certain, though, that they would be re-arrested on stage, and during every Monday

The 'Cat and Mouse Act', introduced in May 1913, prevented hunger striking suffragettes from securing unconditional freedom. Dying suffragettes were released from prison and were recalled after a slight recovery. The poster was designed by the Suffrage Atelier to demonstrate the inhumanity of the Home Secretary's measure.

meeting in July police were waiting at the Pavilion and either Mrs Pankhurst or Annie Kenney was taken back to prison. By August, the leaders were so weak that the authorities slackened their control and the women were allowed freely to address two public meetings. At the same time, an International Medical Congress was taking place at the Albert Hall and outside the conference sandwich boards proclaimed 'The British Government Is Murdering Women'. Shortly afterwards, Mrs Pankhurst and Annie Kenney were allowed to leave England for France.

During this period, the WSPU began to concern itself with an entirely new line of policy. The White Slave Traffic Act had recently been introduced to limit the activities of prostitutes, and Christabel chose this moment to embark on a campaign against prostitution, exposing in great detail the dire effects of venereal disease and advocating chastity for men. Many medical experts gave their opinion and each week a long article on the subject appeared in *The Suffragette*. Eventually the articles were amalgamated in a book, *The Great Scourge And How To Cure It*, which caused considerable controversy and may have been partly responsible, in the autumn of 1913, for Mrs Pankhurst's being detained as an undesirable on Ellis Island before she was allowed to carry out a lecture tour in America.

High-minded as the new policy seemed to be – and it was a cause that many suffragists had taken up during the previous fifty years – there was probably an ulterior motive behind Christabel's exposition. In the 'Piccadilly Flat Case', which was the first trial under the White Slave Traffic Act, the procuress concerned received an extremely mild sentence. The suffragettes were aware that certain high-ranking officials were involved in the scandal and, both in their own paper and in the national press, there were undertones of threatened exposure.

A very positive result of Christabel's articles was the support given to them by the clergy, and from this time onwards the suffragettes adopted the clergy as their allies. Although the women caused considerable nuisance and embarrassment in clerical circles, sending out petitions to all ranks and interrupting services with organised chanting on behalf of their imprisoned friends and leaders, a large section of churchmen lent their support and it was not withdrawn despite the militant outrages in the last desperate months before the suffragettes 'disarmed'.

Although there was nationwide arson and destruction of property, suffragettes in every small town continued to campaign just as they always had done, holding drawing-room meetings, garden parties, selling the paper and advertising their latest policy by means of colourful poster parades. Mild militancy developed in the form of active protests in theatres, restaurants and churches, while the campaign which chiefly concerned the women at headquarters was still to plan the leaders' public appearances and escapes.

In preparation for the return from abroad of Annie Kenney and Mrs Pankhurst, a large bodyguard was trained. Sylvia Pankhurst, who had broken away from the WSPU to run her own Socialist-affiliated campaign in London's East End, had a similar group to protect her known as the 'People's Army'. The 'Cat and Mouse Act' soon became a complete mockery because of the almost unfailing success of these new contingents, who, armed with Indian clubs and following carefully planned strategy, outwitted the police on numerous occasions. Forcible feeding was renewed as a result and prison methods changed considerably.

It was soon discovered that large doses of bromide had been given to suffragette prisoners, and those women who could not be forcibly fed because of heart weakness were not released after hunger striking until so feeble that their health was permanently damaged.

Elaborate measures were taken to arrest Mrs Pankhurst at sea on her return from America in December and a further series of imprisonments and releases followed. Her defiance and refusal to eat, drink or sleep ensured that imprisonment would now last no longer than three days. Once, when on release, she escaped from a guarded house having first announced to crowds assembled below that she would do so. She would not keep herself out of the public eye for any length of time, however, and her appearance on the platform inevitably invited re-arrest.

The most dramatic of these episodes occurred at Glasgow when the platform was surrounded with barbed wire concealed by festoons of flowers, and the bodyguard, dressed in white, sat on stage innocently nursing their Indian clubs beneath their skirts. There was a fight on the platform during which a woman fired a blank shot from a pistol, and in their eagerness to arrest Mrs Pankhurst, her captors tore her clothes and vindictively bruised and mauled her with complete lack of control.

The suffragettes were outraged, and in protest, Mary Richardson slashed Velasquez's portrait, 'The Rokeby Venus' at the National Gallery. She justified her action by saying that she had tried to destroy the picture of the most beautiful woman in mythological history in protest against the Government's destroying Mrs Pankhurst, the most beautiful character in modern history.

Mrs Pankhurst, released under McKenna's act, was allowed to recover at Ethel Smyth's Woking cottage.

Bored by endless police surveillance, she decided to return to London but detectives blocked the way, as, accompanied by nurse and doctor, she tried to enter her car. Exhausted, she fell fainting into Dr Ethel's arms.

DAILY SKETCH.

No. 1,326.—MONDAY, JUNE 9, 1913.   London: 46-47, Shoe-lane, E.C.   Manchester: Withy-grove.   [Registered as a Newspaper.]   ONE HALFPENNY.
Telephones—Editorial and Publishing: 6676 Holborn.   Advertisements: 10,782 Central.

DEATH OF EMILY DAVISON, WHO STOPPED THE KING'S DERBY HORSE, AND IS THE FIRST WOMAN TO GIVE HER LIFE FOR VOTES FOR WOMEN.

The deed which cost Miss Davison her life—the Derby Day incident snapped by a *Daily Sketch* staff photographer. Miss Davison is seen being thrown to the ground, and the King's horse is rolling on his jockey.

Three photographs of the first martyr. Right or wrong she had the courage of her convictions and gave her life for the vote. The third photograph was taken on her release from prison after the hosepipe incident.

A diagram illustrative of the express speed at which a racehorse travels. It was when the King's horse was racing faster than a train that Miss Davison threw herself at it.

Miss Emily Davison is the first woman to die for the cause of votes for women. She never regained consciousness after her wild act on Epsom racecourse during the Derby, and died yesterday afternoon in the Epsom Cottage Hospital. One of the first of the militants, she was often imprisoned, and many times was forcibly fed. Once at Manchester she barricaded her cell, and the authorities hosepiped her through her prison window. On another occasion the prison officials put her in a strait jacket, but she was so slender that she slipped through it. Yet this delicate woman is making all England talk to-day.

Left. Mrs Pankhurst's fate caused national speculation and popular opinion said 'let her die!' Emily Wilding Davison was convinced that one martyr could save the cause and on Derby Day, 4 June 1913, she sacrificed herself by darting on to the racecourse and attempting to stop the King's horse.

In spite of government attempts to cripple the WSPU the public was shown unmistakeable proof of its survival in the moving Emily Wilding Davison funeral procession. A long line of women carrying flowers and dressed in purple, white and black, accompanied the cortège past silent and sorrowful crowds.

Mrs Pankhurst spent the summer of
1913 in and out of prison, occasionally
addressing public meetings when she
managed to elude her guard. In
August she was allowed to visit
France and she then travelled on to
the United States for a lecture tour.

Top Left On one hand public opinion
was outraged and sickened by suffragette destruction and arson; on the
other it deplored the treatment of
suffragette prisoners. A photographer
must have gained access to a site
overlooking the Holloway exercise
yard in order to take this gruelling
picture of hunger strikers.

Bottom Left 'The Government is
murdering women!' Suffragettes
carrying sandwich boards pro-
claiming this message in different
languages, paraded outside the Albert
Hall while the International Medical
Congress was taking place there at
the beginning of August 1913.

On arriving in the United States, Mrs Pankhurst was detained at Ellis Island as an undesirable. Her influential supporter, Mrs Belmont, speedily secured her release through the President and greatly added to Mrs Pankhurst's prestige. Here, Mrs Pankhurst is speaking in Madison Square on 22 October 1913.

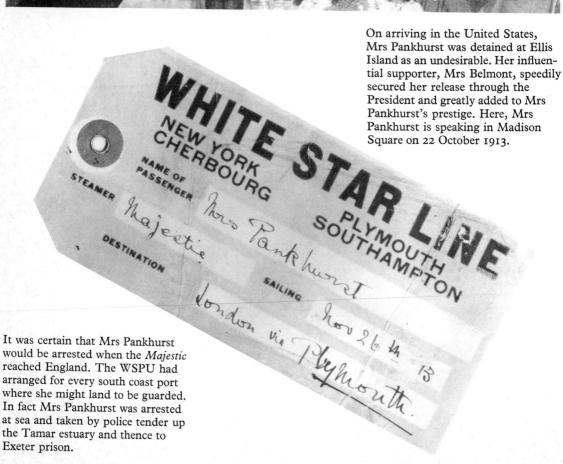

WHITE STAR LINE
NEW YORK
CHERBOURG
PLYMOUTH
SOUTHAMPTON

NAME OF PASSENGER   Mrs Pankhurst

STEAMER   Majestic

DESTINATION   London via Plymouth

SAILING   Nov 26th 13

It was certain that Mrs Pankhurst would be arrested when the *Majestic* reached England. The WSPU had arranged for every south coast port where she might land to be guarded. In fact Mrs Pankhurst was arrested at sea and taken by police tender up the Tamar estuary and thence to Exeter prison.

McKenna's act stopped forcible feeding only
temporarily for it was resumed when suffragettes,
escaping their guards, prevented the act's
enforcement. Clergymen supporting a WSPU
anti-VD campaign, took up other suffragette
causes and protested against prison atrocities. The
Bishop of London investigated cases of alleged
drugging of suffragettes in Holloway.

DETERMINED EFFORT

AGAINST

FORCIBLE FEEDING.

COME IN THOUSANDS TO A

GREAT PROTEST
DEMONSTRATION

OF THE

CLERGY

AT THE

Queen's Hall, Friday, December 5,

at 8 p.m.

CHAIRMAN:

Rt. Rev. BISHOP of KENSINGTON

SUPPORTED BY A PLATFORM OF
Bishops and other influential officials of the
Church, in all parts of the Country.

PRISON TORTURE
MUST CEASE.

All communications to the Rev. J. Drew Roberts, and Rev.
E. A. Morgan, Secretaries, at the Offices of the National Political
League, Bank Buildings, 14, St. James's Street, S.W.

Telephone: 334 Gerrard.

ADMISSION FREE.   Reserved Seats **5/-, 2/6** and **1/-**

The Utopia Press (T.U. and 48 hours), 44, Worship Street, London, E.C.

By 1914 Mrs Pankhurst had been arrested and
released on licence six times. Frequently she
defied the authorities, spoke in public and,
strongly protected by a bodyguard, avoided
arrest. Here she is seen addressing crowds from
the balcony of a Chelsea house before once more
escaping.

"Lest We Forget" Sung At A Fashionable Wedding.

DAILY SKETCH.

No. 1,561.   LONDON, WEDNESDAY, MARCH 11, 1914.   [Registered as a Newspaper.]   ONE HALFPENNY.

ROKEBY VENUS, BOUGHT BY THE NATION FOR £45,000, SLASHED WITH A CHOPPER BY A SUFFRAGETTE IN THE NATIONAL GALLERY.

Mary Richardson in the hands of the police.

The Rokeby "Venus," which cost the nation £45,000—now ruined.

A portrait of Velasquez, by himself.

Lord Curzon being interviewed by the reporters—

After they had waited for two hours.

One of the most dastardly outrages recently attempted by the Suffragists was committed at the National Gallery yesterday morning, when Velasquez's famous £45,000 " Venus and Cupid " was attacked with a hatchet. Before she could be prevented, six or seven cuts were made in the picture, and a piece as big as half-a-crown cut out. Immediately arrested, the woman gave her name as Mary Richardson. She is a well-known Suffragist, and member of the Women's Social and Political Un. The National Gallery, of which Lord Curzon is one of the trustees, was immed ly closed to the public for the day.—(Hanfstaengl.)

The police caught Mrs Pankhurst
again at a meeting in Glasgow on 9
March 1914. After a bloody struggle
on the platform, Mrs Pankhurst
was dragged off by detectives, hit
and manhandled. In London, Mary
Richardson, shocked by news of the
arrest, slashed Velasquez' *Venus* in
the National Gallery.

While all other leading WSPU speakers were under arrest, Mrs Drummond, regardless of prohibitions, held meetings all over the country. On 14 April 1914, in competition with Irish militants who were permitted to address the crowds, Mrs Drummond stole the show by speaking from a dog-cart.

Release of the Furies

Open war is usually prefaced by those sporadic and aimless acts of militancy which bespeak a widespread and extreme unrest. After March 1914, suffragette militancy became noticeably more haphazard and dangerous than before. The outrageous behaviour of the militant women seemed, in contrast to their previously highly organised actions, to be unco-ordinated and anarchic. More pictures were slashed, numerous buildings were destroyed and bombs were discovered in churches.

In Ulster, Irish Unionists were taking up arms and committing outrages but their militancy went relatively unpunished. The suffragettes made this one of their chief complaints and took every opportunity to pester and criticise the Unionist leaders. Mrs Drummond had appeared on the scene again and, defiantly heedless of the new rules banning suffragette outdoor meetings, was travelling up and down the country making witty and forceful speeches. At the reins of a dogcart, charging through Hyde Park, she stole the glory of Ulster Day from the Irishmen who were not banned from speaking there. Why Mrs Drummond managed for so long to avoid arrest may be explained by the fact that she was always on excellent terms with the police. When she was at last taken to court she refused to stay in the dock and kept up a continual flow of invective throughout the proceedings so that no lawyer could be heard. Other suffragettes followed her example at later trials.

Their final attempt at a constitutional protest was a deputation to the King. Since all Mrs Pankhurst's requests for a personal interview were refused, she announced that a mass deputation would go to Buckingham Palace on 21 May 1914. Hundreds of police were recruited to stand guard but Mrs Pankhurst, hidden among the bodyguard, eluded them, slipped through the gates of Constitution Hill just as they were closing and reached the front of the Palace before being arrested. This dramatic arrest may possibly have been a publicity stunt by the police, but at the same time it was excellent

A deputation to the King had been openly announced and women from all over the country came on 21 May 1914 to join the march on Buckingham Palace. Mrs Pankhurst, protected by the bodyguard, is seen here starting out from the house in Grosvenor Place where she had been hiding.

advertisement for the suffragettes. A wild battle followed. The women armed with strange weapons – eggs filled with paint and secateurs for cutting the reins of the police horses – managed for a time to hold their own. Soon, however, they were overcome and hundreds were arrested, while those who were still at liberty embarked on a stone-throwing protest later that evening.

Suffragette security measures were so strict that their plans were seldom discovered, but a careless oversight at the height of the excitement of the deputation led to the police discovering one of their arsenals. Detectives were on the spot when a woman appeared with a basket of stones covered with cabbage leaves, and this led to other discoveries. The WSPU headquarters were once again raided and now at last, Grace Roe was arrested. She was imprisoned and forcibly fed before being convicted, and from then on every possible measure was taken to destroy suffragette morale both inside and outside prison. McKenna admitted that the country was faced with a phenomenon absolutely unparalleled in history and the press complained about the militants' 'Midsummer Madness'. Further personal attempts were made to petition the King and, as a joke, a man who had nothing to do with the suffragettes, got into the Palace. Once inside, he changed his clothes for a suit he found there, and was later discovered wandering aimlessly and arrested. The public deplored this lack of respect for royalty and longed for a peaceful solution to the suffragette question.

In June 1914, Asquith did at last consent to receive a deputation from Sylvia Pankhurst's East End Federation, but the WSPU was sceptical of Asquith's *volte face* and refused to make any concessions towards a settlement. Finally, when the situation was at its most intolerable, war with Germany was declared. An amnesty was granted to all suffragette prisoners and Mrs Pankhurst, calling a truce, put all her existing forces towards assisting the country in the war effort.

Cordons of police surrounded the
Palace but even so some women
managed to break through the lines
and make a dash for the gates.

Mrs Pankhurst and her bodyguard managed to slip through the gates at Constitution Hill just as they were being closed. They made for the Palace and as she arrived at its gates, Mrs Pankhurst was seized by the inspector who had evidently been posted there to make a dramatic arrest.

This woman under arrest, dishevelled and dejected, has a certain timeless quality about her appearance.

As on Black Friday, women refused to be repulsed and consequently they were mauled and injured before finally being arrested. The picture shows Mrs Eleanor Higginson, from Preston, screaming as her arms are being twisted by the police.

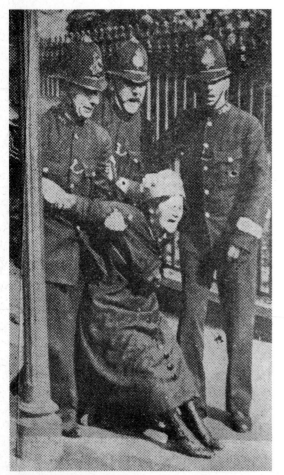

News placards, which appeared after the Buckingham Palace assault, proclaimed the shocking scene and its consequences.

ARMED WOMEN BESIEGE THE KING

The Globe
EDITION

MAN IN THE "PALACE: ASTOUNDING COURT STORY

The Globe
B 6 14

ROWDY SCENES BEFORE THE KING & QUEEN

WESTMINSTER
FINAL EDITION.

SUFFRAGETTES BURN ANOTHER CHURCH

Evening News 6.30

...TTES BATONED BY POLICE

Evening News 6.30

...TTE RAID ON THE PALACE: WILD SCENES

WESTMINSTER
FINAL EDITION.

A stone-throwing attack which followed the Buckingham Palace deputation, and incriminating discoveries in a Maida Vale flat, led to a police raid on suffragette headquarters. Grace Roe was at last identified and arrested. Here she is leaving Lincoln's Inn House giving a reassuring glance to supporters standing by.

"The Suffragette," June 5, 1914.   The   Registered at the G.P.O. as a Newspaper

Suffragette

Edited by Christabel Pankhurst.   The Official Organ of the
Women's Social and Political Union

No. 86—Vol. III.   FRIDAY, JUNE 5, 1914.   Price 1d. Weekly (Post Free 1½d.)

WOMEN
DRUGGED
AND
TORTURED
IN
PRISON

Reacting to the unco-operative behaviour of suffragettes, the prison authorities became progressively more frustrated and vindictive. Mrs Pankhurst was stripped naked when she refused to be searched. Other women who resisted forcible feeding were held down by wardresses to undergo the operation when doses of sedative were administered.

Sylvia Pankhurst left the
WSPU in 1913 to run a
parallel campaign in
London's East End. In
June 1914 she too was
suffering after imprison-
ment but, in the absence of
WSPU leaders, Sylvia
prevailed on her loyal
followers to convey her in
an invalid chair to West-
minster to make an
individual plea.

The alarming events of
previous months and
Sylvia's forceful action
persuaded Asquith to
receive a deputation from
the East End. These six
women ultimately met the
Prime Minister face to face
on 20 June 1914 and ex-
tracted from him the
statement that votes for
women was a possibility.

Postscript: Women's War Effort

It was as though the nine gruelling years of the suffragette campaign were merely a preparation for what Mrs Pankhurst was to do after 1914. Although still suffering from the effects of her hunger strikes, she had never worked with such amazing strength and absolute assurance as she did in those early years of the war.

It is assumed today that women automatically volunteered for service to their country. They needed to be persuaded and organised, however, as did the men who were reluctant to allow women to take over their jobs so that they would be free to fight. Once again Christabel and Mrs Pankhurst worked together as closely as they had done in the early days – Christabel advocating policy and Mrs Pankhurst expounding it at huge patriotic meetings up and down the country.

In June 1915, at a moment of extreme crisis brought on by a munitions shortage, Lloyd George, in his capacity of Minister of Munitions, called on the suffragettes to organise a demonstration that would initially produce a voluntary brigade of women to begin immediate work in the munitions factories. Mrs Pankhurst sent out a 'Call to Women', and within a matter of days thousands sent in their names. Then, in public proof of their willingness to work for the country, they joined together in a huge organised procession on 17 July.

The Times, commenting on the demonstration, said: 'It reveals the spirit of our women and it is a striking example of their perception that all social and political values will be determined by the way they have stood the test of War.' It was inevitable that the vote would be given to women in 1918 when a new extension of the franchise was brought in, but the 1918 measure did not allow women under thirty to vote. Not until the 'Flapper Vote' of 1928 were all women over the age of twenty-one put on the electoral roll. It was in that year that Mrs Pankhurst died, as the movement which had begun as a family enterprise and, once grown, had arguably saved the country, finally went into retirement with all its aims achieved.

The outbreak of war in August 1914 brought militancy to a timely close. An amnesty was declared, all suffragette prisoners were released and Mrs Pankhurst placed the WSPU's resources at the service of the country. Production of 'The Suffragette' stopped temporarily but it reappeared in patriotic guise in October 1915.

"Britannia," October 15, 1915.

FOR KING · FOR COUNTRY · FOR FREEDOM

Britannia

With which is incorporated
"THE SUFFRAGETTE"

Official Organ of the Women's Social
and Political Union

Edited by CHRISTABEL PANKHURST

No. 1. Vol. V.   FRIDAY, OCTOBER 15, 1915   Price 1d. Weekly (Post Free 1½d.)

Still more majestic shalt thou rise,
  More dreadful from each foreign stroke;
As the loud blast that tears the skies
  Serves but to root thy native oak.

Thee haughty tyrants ne'er shall tame;
  All their attempts to haul thee down
Will but arouse thy generous flame,
  And work their woe, but thy renown.

From "Rule Britannia," by James Thomson.

As soon as Mrs Pankhurst had recovered sufficiently from the effects of imprisonment she embarked on a tour of the country addressing large meetings, explaining the German peril and advocating conscription and rationing. Here a woman is seen advertising this campaign.

At the start of the war, strong male antagonism towards women doing their work delayed an efficient recruitment programme and Mrs Pankhurst's patriotic speeches did much to allay discontent among workers. In the picture she is seen pacifying a group of Welsh miners who had threatened to strike.

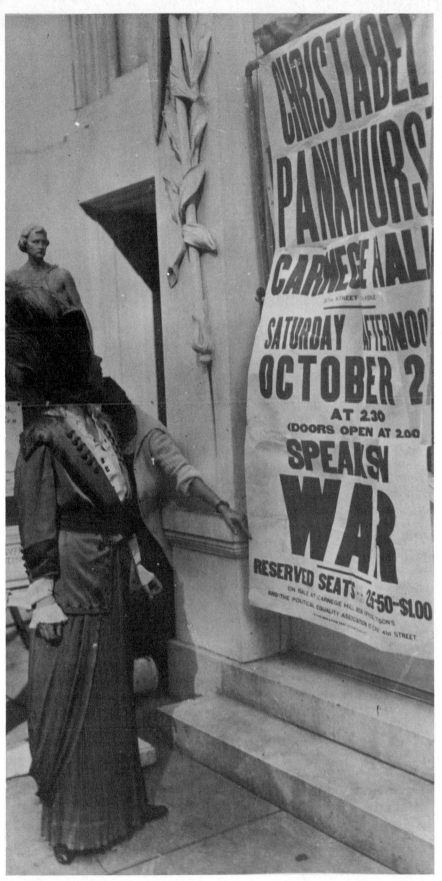

From the start of the war the suffragettes recognised the importance of America to the Allied cause. In turn, the suffragette leaders made propaganda visits to the United States. Here Christabel stands by a poster advertising her Carnegie Hall meeting in October 1915.

During the munitions crisis
of July 1915 the King
suggested to Lloyd George
that Mrs Pankhurst should
organise a patriotic demonstration to enlist women
for work in the munitions
factories. Here Mrs.
Drummond and Lloyd
George, formerly old
enemies, cheerfully unite in
the patriotic effort.

An impressive procession
achieved a magnificent
response. At tables, posted
along the route, thousands
signed on for recruitment.